THE

PICTURE PUZZLE
CHALLENGE

THIS IS A CARLTON BOOK

Published by Carlton Books Limited
20 Mortimer Street
London W1T 3JW

ISBN: 978-1-84732-504-4

10 9 8 7 6 5 4

Printed in Singapore

All images supplied by Jupiter Images

Editorial: Roland Hall
Puzzles devised by Tim Dedopulos
Design: Adam Wright
Production: Claire Hayward
Picture Research: Stephen O'Kelly

THE PICTURE PUZZLE CHALLENGE

CARLTON
BOOKS

CONTENTS

Introduction: Solving Photo Puzzles

Photographic puzzles give us something missing from our daily lives – a measurable test of our powers of observation. Sight is our most important sense, and our ability to observe determines how much we can benefit from it. The puzzles in this book will offer you an optical workout, sharpen up your visual acuity, and – best of all – let you see how well you're doing. Each category starts out easy to break you in gently, and gradually works up to fiendishly tough for a special challenge.

Success with photo puzzles involves combining scrutiny with a dash of creative thinking. The human eye is great at recognizing patterns and structures. Easier puzzles will make use of this, breaking patterning, switching colours and changing spaces. Try flicking your eyes quickly back and forth, and let them find the solutions for you.

Tougher puzzles attempt to avoid this mental circuitry. As the challenges get harder, patterns may be twisted slightly, or left alone entirely. Colour changes will be subtle. To tackle the hardest puzzles, look away from obvious pattern areas into backgrounds or details, and cross-reference methodically.

Most importantly though, don't give up – and have fun! A whole world of puzzle delight awaits you.

ENIGMAS

These puzzles will test your lateral thinking to the extremes. These images will appear unfamiliar, even confusing. Some are familiar objects photographed in such a way as to appear strange, such as extreme close up; others are less familiar, reproduced plainly. Your job is to identify the item. Good luck!

Puzzle 1 – What are you looking at?

Answer on page 152

Puzzle 2 – What are you looking at?

Answer on page 152

Puzzle 3 – What are you looking at?

Answer on page 152

Puzzle 4 – What are you looking at?

Answer on page 152

Puzzle 5 – What are you looking at?

Answer on page 152

Puzzle 6 – What are you looking at?

Answer on page 152

Puzzle 7 – What are you looking at?

Answer on page 152

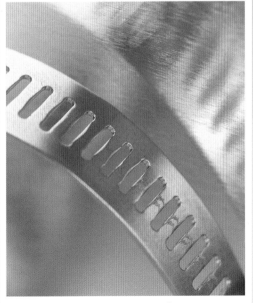

Puzzle 8 – What are you looking at?

Answer on page 152

Puzzle 9 – What are you looking at?

Answer on page 152

Puzzle 10 – What are you looking at?

Answer on page 152

Puzzle 11 – What are you looking at?

Answer on page 152

Puzzle 12 – What are you looking at?

Answer on page 152

Answer on page 152

Puzzle 13 – What are you looking at?

Answer on page 152

Puzzle 14 – What are you looking at?

Answer on page 152

Puzzle 15 – What are you looking at?

Answer on page 152

Puzzle 16 – What are you looking at?

Answer on page 152

Puzzle 17 – What are you looking at?

Answer on page 152

Puzzle 18 – What are you looking at?

Answer on page 152

Puzzle 19 – What are you looking at?

Answer on page 152

Puzzle 20 – What are you looking at?

Puzzle 21 – What are you looking at?

Puzzle 22 – What are you looking at?

Answer on page 152

Answer on page 152

Puzzle 23 – What are you looking at?

Puzzle 24 – What are you looking at?

Answer on page 152

Answer on page 152

MISSING MONUMENTS

A tricky test of your cultural IQ, these puzzles all show a world-famous location. Unfortunately, we have used the latest digital technologies to remove that place from the photograph! Working from just the background scenery and other clues, are you able to figure out the identity of the missing monument?

Puzzle 25 – Which famous landmark has been removed?

Answer on page 153

Puzzle 26 – Which famous landmark has been removed?

Answer on page 153

Puzzle 27 – Which famous landmark has been removed?

Answer on page 153

Puzzle 28 – Which famous landmark has been removed?

Answer on page 153

Puzzle 29 – Which famous landmark has been removed?

Answer on page 153

Puzzle 30 – Which famous landmark has been removed?

Answer on page 153

Medium

Answer on page 153

Puzzle 31 – Which famous landmark has been removed?

Answer on page 153

Puzzle 32 – Which famous landmark has been removed?

21

Puzzle 33 — Which famous landmark has been removed?

Answer on page 154

Puzzle 34 — Which famous landmark has been removed?

Answer on page 154

Answer on page 154

Puzzle 35 – Which famous landmark has been removed?

Answer on page 154

Puzzle 36 – Which famous landmark has been removed?

Puzzle 37 — Which famous landmark has been removed?

Answer on page 154

Puzzle 38 — Which famous landmark has been removed?

Answer on page 154

Puzzle 39 – Which famous landmark has been removed?

Answer on page 154

Puzzle 40 – Which famous landmark has been removed?

Answer on page 154

SCRAMBLERS

Scramblers are a high-octane test of your brain's pattern-matching abilities. These photographs have been broken down into a number of chunks, and shuffled around randomly. You'll have to use all your visual skills to reconstruct the original image in your mind, so that you can identify the item it shows.

Puzzle 41 – What are you looking at?

Answer on page 155

Puzzle 42 – What are you looking at?

Answer on page 156

Puzzle 43 – What are you looking at?

Answer on page 157

Puzzle 44 – What are you looking at?

Answer on page 158

Puzzle 45 – What are you looking at?

Answer on page 155

Puzzle 46 – What are you looking at?

Answer on page 156

30

Puzzle 47 – What are you looking at?

Answer on page 157

Puzzle 48 – What are you looking at?

Answer on page 158

Answer on page 155

Puzzle 49 – What are you looking at?

Answer on page 156

Puzzle 50 – What are you looking at?

Answer on page 158

Puzzle 51 – What are you looking at?

Answer on page 157

Puzzle 52 – What are you looking at?

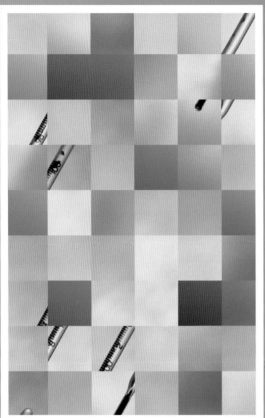

Puzzle 53 – What are you looking at?

Answer on page 155

Puzzle 54 – What are you looking at?

Answer on page 156

Hard

Puzzle 55 — What are you looking at?

Answer on page 157

Puzzle 56 — What are you looking at?

Answer on page 158

Puzzle 57 – What are you looking at?

Answer on page 155

Puzzle 58 – What are you looking at?

Answer on page 156

Puzzle 59 – What are you looking at?

Answer on page 157

Puzzle 60 – What are you looking at?

Answer on page 158

Puzzle 61 — What are you looking at?

Answer on page 155

Puzzle 62 — What are you looking at?

Answer on page 156

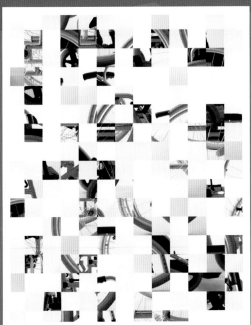

Answer on page 157

Puzzle 63 – What are you looking at?

Answer on page 158

Puzzle 64 – What are you looking at?

SCENES

In these puzzles, we have hidden
a number of changes within a
traditional photograph showing
a scene of some sort. The original,
unaltered photograph is shown next
to the changed version so you can
compare the two. Remember to look
for pattern changes in the easier
puzzles, and detail changes
in harder ones!

Puzzle 65 – Can you spot 7 differences between the two images?

Answer on page 159

Puzzle 66 – Can you spot 7 differences between the two images?

Answer on page 160

Puzzle 67 – Can you spot 6 differences between the two images?

Answer on page 161

Puzzle 68 – Can you spot 5 differences between the two images?

Answer on page 162

Puzzle 69 – Can you spot 6 differences between the two images?

Answer on page 163

Puzzle 70 – Can you spot 6 differences between the two images?

Answer on page 164

Puzzle 71 – Can you spot 7 differences between the two images?

Answer on page 165

Puzzle 72 – Can you spot 7 differences between the two images?

Answer on page 166

Puzzle 73 – Can you spot 7 differences between the two images?

Answer on page 167

50

Puzzle 74 – Can you spot 6 differences between the two images?

Answer on page 168

Puzzle 75 – Can you spot 7 differences between the two images?

Answer on page 159

Puzzle 76 – Can you spot 7 differences between the two images?

Answer on page 160

Puzzle 77 – Can you spot 7 differences between the two images?

Answer on page 161

Puzzle 78 – Can you spot 5 differences between the two images?

Answer on page 162

Puzzle 79 – Can you spot 6 differences between the two images?

Puzzle 80 – Can you spot 7 differences between the two images?

Answer on page 164

Puzzle 81 – Can you spot 6 differences between the two images?

Answer on page 165

Puzzle 82 – Can you spot 6 differences between the two images?

Answer on page 166

Puzzle 83 – Can you spot 6 differences between the two images?

Puzzle 84 – Can you spot 7 differences between the two images?

Answer on page 168

Puzzle 85 – Can you spot 7 differences between the two images?

Answer on page 159

Puzzle 86 – Can you spot 6 differences between the two images?

Answer on page 160

Puzzle 87 – Can you spot 7 differences between the two images?

Answer on page 161

Puzzle 88 – Can you spot 6 differences between the two images?

Answer on page 162

Puzzle 89 – Can you spot 7 differences between the two images?

Answer on page 163

Puzzle 90 – Can you spot 6 differences between the two images?

Answer on page 164

Puzzle 91 – Can you spot 7 differences between the two images?

Answer on page 165

Puzzle 92 – Can you spot 7 differences between the two images?

Answer on page 166

Puzzle 93 – Can you spot 7 differences between the two images?

Answer on page 167

Puzzle 94 – Can you spot 7 differences between the two images?

Answer on page 168

Puzzle 95 – Can you spot 7 differences between the two images?

Answer on page 159

Puzzle 96 – Can you spot 7 differences between the two images?

Answer on page 160

Puzzle 97 – Can you spot 6 differences between the two images?

Answer on page 161

Puzzle 98 – Can you spot 7 differences between the two images?

Answer on page 162

Puzzle 99 – Can you spot 7 differences between the two images?

Answer on page 163

Puzzle 100 – Can you spot 7 differences between the two images?

Answer on page 164

Puzzle 101 – Can you spot 7 differences between the two images?

Puzzle 102 – Can you spot 6 differences between the two images?

Answer on page 166

Puzzle 103 – Can you spot 6 differences between the two images?

Answer on page 167

Puzzle 104 – Can you spot 8 differences between the two images?

Answer on page 168

Puzzle 105 – Can you spot 7 differences between the two images?

Answer on page 159

Puzzle 106 – Can you spot 8 differences between the two images?

Answer on page 160

Puzzle 107 – Can you spot 7 differences between the two images?

Answer on page 161

Hard

Puzzle 108 – Can you spot 6 differences between the two images?

Answer on page 162

85

Puzzle 109 – Can you spot 7 differences between the two images?

Answer on page 163

Puzzle 110 – Can you spot 7 differences between the two images?

Answer on page 164

Puzzle 111 – Can you spot 6 differences between the two images?

Answer on page 165

Puzzle 112 – Can you spot 7 differences between the two images?

Answer on page 166

Puzzle 113 – Can you spot 6 differences between the two images?

Answer on page 167

Puzzle 114 – Can you spot 6 differences between the two images?

Answer on page 168

Puzzle 115 – Can you spot 7 differences between the two images?

Answer on page 159

Puzzle 116 – Can you spot 6 differences between the two images?

Answer on page 160

Puzzle 117 – Can you spot 6 differences between the two images?

Answer on page 161

Puzzle 118 – Can you spot 5 differences between the two images?

Answer on page 162

Puzzle 119 – Can you spot 7 differences between the two images?

Answer on page 163

Puzzle 120 – Can you spot 6 differences between the two images?

Answer on page 164

Puzzle 121 – Can you spot 5 differences between the two images?

Answer on page 165

Puzzle 122 – Can you spot 6 differences between the two images?

Answer on page 166

TEXTURES

Texture photographs focus on repetitive visual structures, and the elements – fruit, cracks in a rock, sweets – are often jumbled around, without much underlying order. They pose a special Spot The Difference challenge, because they offer little pattern for the eye to pick out. Are you up to the task?

Puzzle 123 – Can you spot 6 differences between the two images?

Answer on page 168

Puzzle 124 – Can you spot 9 differences between the two images?

Answer on page 167

Puzzle 125 – Can you spot 7 differences between the two images?

Answer on page 169

Puzzle 126 – Can you spot 6 differences between the two images?

Answer on page 170

Puzzle 127 – Can you spot 8 differences between the two images?

Answer on page 171

Puzzle 128 – Can you spot 5 differences between the two images?

Puzzle 129 – Can you spot 7 differences between the two images?

Answer on page 173

Puzzle 130 – Can you spot 6 differences between the two images?

Answer on page 174

Puzzle 131 – Can you spot 8 differences between the two images?

Answer on page 175

Puzzle 132 – Can you spot 6 differences between the two images?

Answer on page 176

Puzzle 133 – Can you spot 8 differences between the two images?

Answer on page 169

Puzzle 134 – Can you spot 6 differences between the two images?

Answer on page 170

Puzzle 135 – Can you spot 9 differences between the two images?

Answer on page 171

114

Puzzle 136 – Can you spot 10 differences between the two images?

Answer on page 172

Puzzle 137 – Can you spot 9 differences between the two images?

Answer on page 173

Puzzle 138 – Can you spot 10 differences between the two images?

Puzzle 139 – Can you spot 9 differences between the two images?

Answer on page 175

Puzzle 140 – Can you spot 10 differences between the two images?

Puzzle 141 – Can you spot 9 differences between the two images?

Answer on page 169

Puzzle 142 – Can you spot 7 differences between the two images?

Answer on page 170

Puzzle 143 – Can you spot 9 differences between the two images?

Answer on page 171

Puzzle 144 – Can you spot 9 differences between the two images?

Answer on page 172

Puzzle 145 – Can you spot 10 differences between the two images?

Answer on page 173

Puzzle 146 – Can you spot 9 differences between the two images?

Answer on page 174

Puzzle 147 – Can you spot 10 differences between the two images?

Answer on page 175

Puzzle 148 – Can you spot 9 differences between the two images?

Answer on page 176

Puzzle149 – Can you spot 9 differences between the two images?

Answer on page 169

Puzzle 150 – Can you spot 9 differences between the two images?

Answer on page 170

Puzzle 151 – Can you spot 10 differences between the two images?

Answer on page 171

Hard

Puzzle 152 – Can you spot 9 differences between the two images?

Puzzle 153 – Can you spot 8 differences between the two images?

Answer on page 173

Puzzle 154 – Can you spot 10 differences between the two images?

Answer on page 174

Puzzle 155 – Can you spot 8 differences between the two images?

Answer on page 175

Puzzle 156 – Can you spot 10 differences between the two images?

Answer on page 176

Puzzle 157 – Can you spot 10 differences between the two images?

Answer on page 169

Puzzle 158 – Can you spot 9 differences between the two images?

Answer on page 170

Puzzle 159 – Can you spot 10 differences between the two images?

Answer on page 171

Puzzle 160 – Can you spot 10 differences between the two images?

Answer on page 172

Puzzle 161 – Can you spot 9 differences between the two images?

Answer on page 173

Puzzle 162 – Can you spot 10 differences between the two images?

Answer on page 174

Puzzle 163 – Can you spot 9 differences between the two images?

Answer on page 175

Puzzle 164 – Can you spot 10 differences between the two images?

Answer on page 176

Puzzle 165 – Can you spot 9 differences between the two images?

Answer on page 169

Puzzle 166 – Can you spot 10 differences between the two images?

Answer on page 170

Puzzle 167 – Can you spot 10 differences between the two images?

Answer on page 171

Puzzle 168 – Can you spot 7 differences between the two images?

Answer on page 172

Puzzle 169 – Can you spot 8 differences between the two images?

Answer on page 173

Puzzle 170 – Can you spot 10 differences between the two images?

Answer on page 174

ANSWERS

ANSWERS

Puzzle **1** Scissors
Puzzle **2** Grater
Puzzle **3** Wheel
Puzzle **4** Fossil
Puzzle **5** Copper brush
Puzzle **6** Wire wool
Puzzle **7** Tin can
Puzzle **8** Fastening clamp
Puzzle **9** Comb
Puzzle **10** Cork
Puzzle **11** Picture frames
Puzzle **12** Noodles

Puzzle **13** Security door
Puzzle **14** Bread
Puzzle **15** Paintball ammunition
Puzzle **16** Pipe organ
Puzzle **17** Paint brush and oil knife
Puzzle **18** Telegraph pad
Puzzle **19** Desert rocks
Puzzle **20** Razor
Puzzle **21** Loudspeaker
Puzzle **22** Beer glass
Puzzle **23** Christsas tree
Puzzle **24** Snowy cable

ANSWERS

25 – The Chrysler Building, New York, NY, USA

29 – Tower of Pisa, Italy

26 – The Jefferson Memorial, Washington, DC, USA

30 – Toronto Skydome, Canada

27 – Mount Rushmore, USA

31 – Tower of London, England

28 – Gizeh, Egypt

32 – Vatican Square, Rome, Italy

ANSWERS

33 – Easter Island

34 – Taj Mahal, India

35 – Eiffel Tower, France

36 – Golden Gate Bridge, USA

37 – Jin Mao Tower, Singapore

38 – Neuschwandstein, Germany

39 – Kyongbokkung Palace, Korea

40 – Rosenborg Castle, Denmark

41

45

49

53

57

61

ANSWERS

42

54

46

58

50

62

43

47

52

55

59

63

ANSWERS

44

56

48

60

51

64

95

5

105

35

115

ANSWERS

66

96

76

106

86

116

97

7

107

7

117

ANSWERS

68

98

78

108

88

118

99

109

119

ANSWERS

70

100

80

110

90

120

71

101

81

111

91

121

ANSWERS

72

102

82

112

92

122

ANSWERS

3

103

83

113

93

124

ANSWERS

84

114

94

123

104

74

125

149

133

157

141

165

ANSWERS

126

150

134

158

142

166

127

151

135

159

143

167

ANSWERS

128

152

136

160

144

168

ANSWERS

129

153

137

161

145

169

173

ANSWERS

130

154

138

162

146

170

81

155

39

163

147

ANSWERS

132

156

140

164

148